VOLUME 131

HAL•LEONARD

Piano Play-Along

AUDIO
ACCESS
INCLUDED

The Piano Guys
WONDERS

CONTENTS

To access audio visit:
www.halleonard.com/mylibrary

Enter Code
4073-8966-0200-2485

Audio Arrangements by The Piano Guys

ISBN 978-1-4950-0973-0

DISTRIBUTED BY

HAL•LEONARD®

7777 W. BLUEMOUND RD. P.O. BOX 13819 MILWAUKEE, WI 53213

Visit Hal Leonard Online at
www.halleonard.com

Visit The Piano Guys at:
thepianoguys.com

As performed by The Piano Guys

STORY OF MY LIFE

Words and Music by JAMIE SCOTT,
JOHN HENRY RYAN, JULIAN BUNETTA,
HARRY STYLES, LIAM PAYNE,
LOUIS TOMLINSON, NIALL HORAN
and ZAIN MALIK
Arranged by STEVEN SHARP NELSON
and AL VAN DER BEEK

Moderately fast

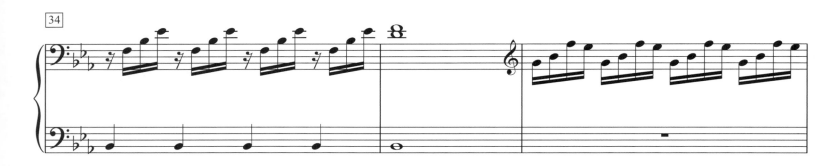

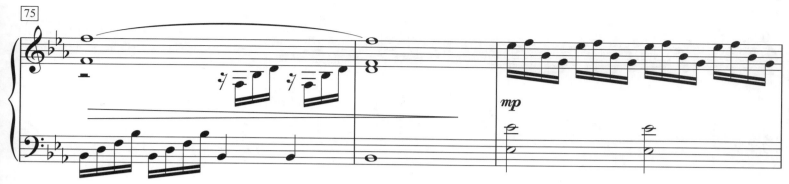

9

As performed by The Piano Guys

LET IT GO
from Disney's Animated Feature FROZEN
Inspired by Concerto No. 4 in F Minor, Op. 8, RV297, "Winter" by Antonio Vivaldi

Music and Lyrics by KRISTEN ANDERSON-LOPEZ
and ROBERT LOPEZ
Arranged by AL VAN DER BEEK,
JON SCHMIDT and STEVEN SHARP NELSON

Moderately fast

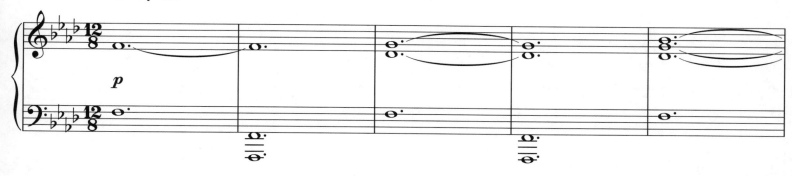

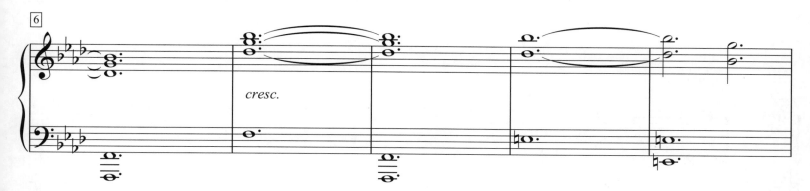

As performed by The Piano Guys

ANTS MARCHING/ODE TO JOY

Inspired by the "Ode To Joy" melody from
Symphony No. 9 in D Minor, Op. 125 by Ludwig van Beethoven

Words and Music by
DAVID J. MATTHEWS
Arranged by AL VAN DER BEEK,
JON SCHMIDT and STEVEN SHARP NELSON

Moderately fast

Mute piano strings with L.H.

22

Mute strings with R.H.

23

Na, na, na, na, _____ na, na, na, na, na,

As performed by The Piano Guys

FATHER'S EYES

By AL VAN DER BEEK
and STEVEN SHARP NELSON

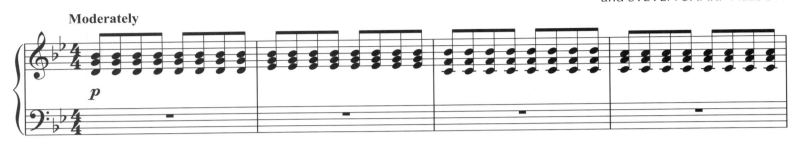

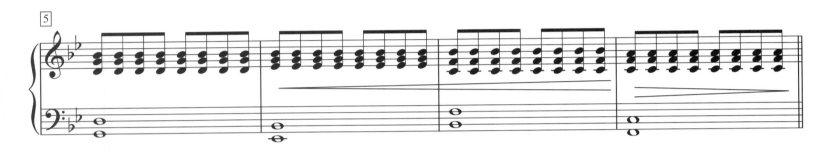

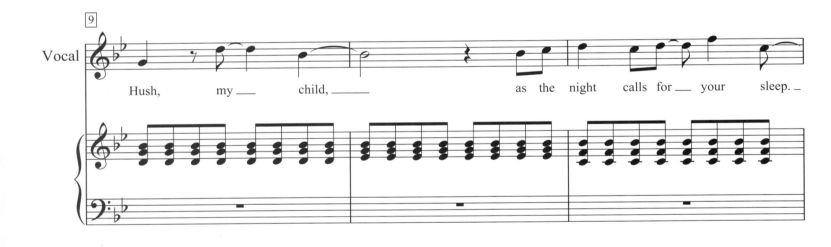

Hush, my ___ child, ___ as the night calls for ___ your sleep. ___

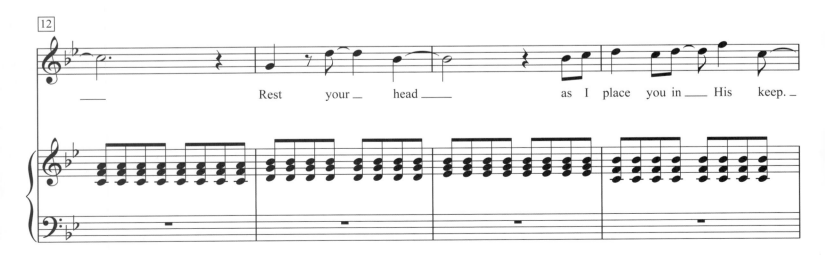

___ Rest your ___ head ___ as I place you in ___ His keep. ___

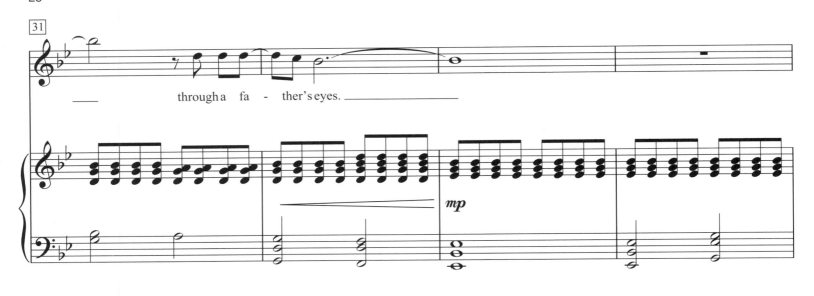

through a fa - ther's eyes.

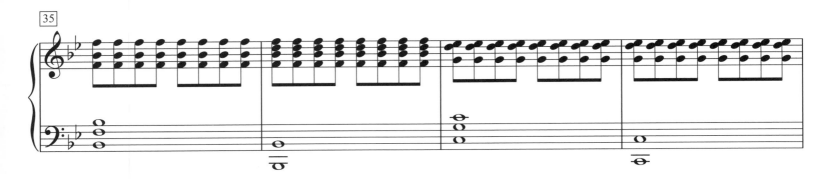

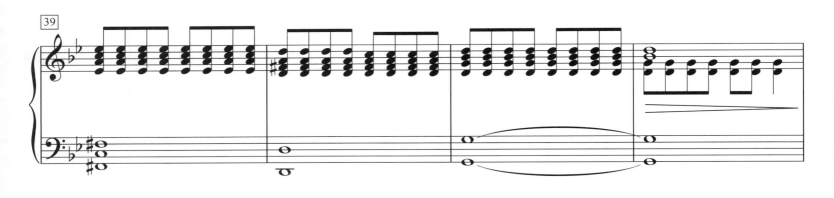

Da, da, da, ___ da, da, ___ da, da. _____

Da, da, da, ___ da, da, ___ da, da, ___ ah. _____

Oh, _____ ooh, ooh, ___ ooh, _____ through a fa-

- ther's eyes.

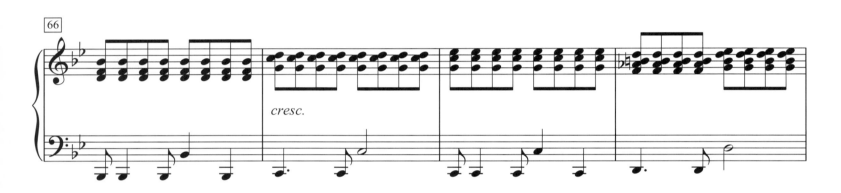

cresc.

Hush, my ___ child, ___ as the night comes for ___ your sleep. ___

Rest your ___ head ___ as I place you in ___ His keep. ___

Through a fa-

- ther's eyes. ___ Through a fa-

ther's eyes.

On - ly through our Fa - ther's

eyes.

As performed by The Piano Guys

SUMMER JAM

By JON SCHMIDT
and STEVEN SHARP NELSON

Moderately

As performed by The Piano Guys

KUNG FU PIANO: CELLO ASCENDS

Based upon and inspired by Frederick Chopin's Prelude Op. 28 No. 20 in C minor

"Oogway Ascends"
By HANS ZIMMER,
JOHN POWELL and HENRY JACKMAN
Arranged by AL VAN DER BEEK,
JON SCHMIDT and STEVEN SHARP NELSON

Moderately slow, expressively

As performed by The Piano Guys

BATMAN EVOLUTION

Arranged by AL VAN DER BEEK
and STEVEN SHARP NELSON

BATMAN THEME
By DANNY ELFMAN

BATMAN THEME
Words and Music by NEAL HEFTI

50

LIKE A DOG CHASING CARS
Composed by HANS ZIMMER
and JAMES NEWTON HOWARD

As performed by The Piano Guys

DON'T YOU WORRY CHILD

Words and Music by STEVE ANGELLO,
AXEL HEDFORS, SEBASTIAN INGROSSO,
MICHEL ZITRON and MARTIN LINDSTROM
Arranged by AL VAN DER BEEK,
STEVEN SHARP NELSON, JON SCHMIDT
and SHWETA SUBRAM

Moderately fast

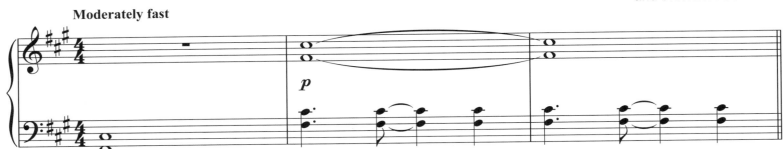

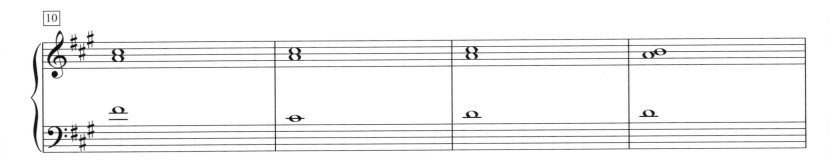

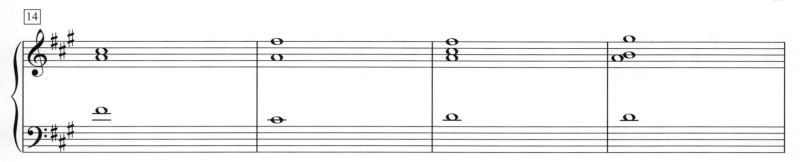

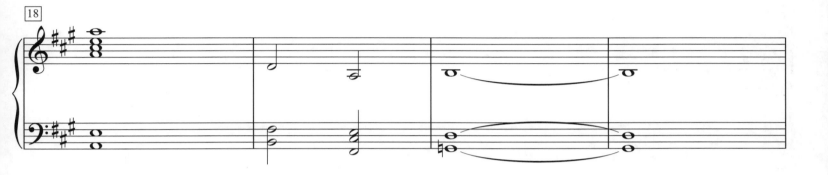

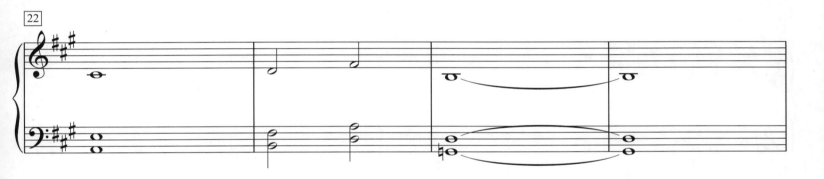

As performed by The Piano Guys

HOME

Inspired by "Going Home," *Largo* melody from Dvořák's *New World Symphony*

Words and Music by GREG HOLDEN
and DREW PEARSON
Arranged by AL VAN DER BEEK,
JON SCHMIDT and STEVEN SHARP NELSON

half pedal

As performed by The Piano Guys

THE MISSION/HOW GREAT THOU ART

THE MISSION
from the Motion Picture THE MISSION
Music by ENNIO MORRICONE
Arranged by JON SCHMIDT,
AL VAN DER BEEK and STEVEN SHARP NELSON

HOW GREAT THOU ART
Words by STUART K. HINE
Swedish Folk Melody Adapted and Arranged by
STUART K. HINE
Arranged by JON SCHMIDT,
AL VAN DER BEEK and STEVEN SHARP NELSON

Slowly, expressively

As performed by The Piano Guys

BECAUSE OF YOU

By AL VAN DER BEEK
and STEVEN SHARP NELSON

Moderately fast

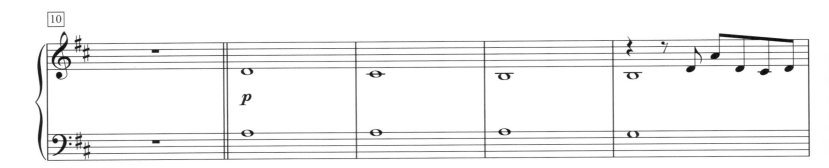

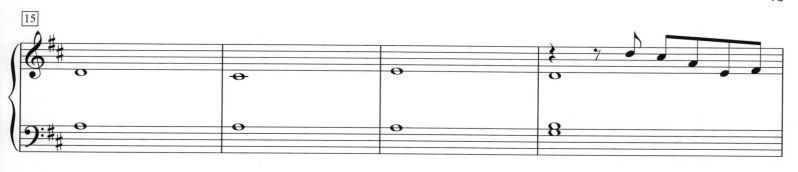

As performed by The Piano Guys

PICTURES AT AN EXHIBITION

By MODEST MUSSORGSKY
Arranged by AL VAN DER BEEK
and STEVEN SHARP NELSON

Moderately fast